Why AI Will Not Eliminate Software Engineering Jobs

By Mohammad Zaripour

Copyright

© 2024 Mohammad Zaripour. All rights reserved.

No part of this book may be reproduced, distributed, or transmitted in any form or by any means, including photocopying, recording, or other electronic or mechanical methods, without the prior written permission of the publisher, except in the case of brief quotations embodied in critical reviews and certain other noncommercial uses permitted by copyright law.

Published by KDP Kindle Direct Publishing

About Author:

Mohammad Zaripour is a Canada-based assistive technology activist. Mohammad's background is in project and business management. He graduated from Carleton University in Ottawa, Canada, in the field of systems and computer engineering

Abstract:

In a world where artificial intelligence (AI) is rapidly advancing, many people fear that AI will take over human jobs, including those in software engineering. This book, "Why AI Will Not Eliminate Software Engineering Jobs," aims to dispel these fears by exploring the unique value and irreplaceable skills that human software engineers bring to the table.

Software engineering is a field that requires creativity, critical thinking, problem-solving, and a deep understanding of human needs and behaviors. While AI can automate repetitive tasks and enhance productivity, it cannot replicate the nuanced and innovative thinking that human engineers provide. This book delves into the symbiotic relationship between AI and software engineers, showing how they can work together to achieve greater efficiency and innovation.

Through real-world examples and expert insights, the book highlights areas where AI excels and where human engineers are indispensable. It discusses the limitations of AI, the importance of human oversight, and the evolving role of software engineers in an AI-augmented world. Readers will learn about the new opportunities that AI creates for software engineers, including the development of AI-driven applications, ethical considerations, and the continuous need for human creativity and adaptability.

"Why AI Will Not Eliminate Software Engineering Jobs" provides a balanced perspective, reassuring software engineers and aspiring professionals that their skills will remain crucial in the future job market. It emphasizes the importance of lifelong learning and adapting to technological changes while maintaining the human touch that makes software engineering a unique and valuable profession.

By Mohammad Zaripour

Table of content

Introduction 7

Chapter 1 12

Chapter 2 43

Chapter 3 65

Chapter 4 76

Chapter 5 89

Chapter 6 100

Chapter 7 112

Conclusion: 125

Appendix 130

By Mohammad Zaripour

Introduction

By Mohammad Zaripour

Introduction

The Rise of AI

Artificial intelligence (AI) is no longer just a futuristic concept found in sci-fi movies. Today, AI is a powerful tool transforming many industries, from healthcare and finance to manufacturing and entertainment. AI technologies, like machine learning and deep learning, can analyze vast amounts of data, recognize patterns, and even make decisions. This rapid advancement has led to significant improvements in efficiency and productivity.

Common Fears and Misconceptions

With these advancements, however, comes a wave of fear and uncertainty. Many people worry that AI will take over human jobs, leaving them unemployed and obsolete. This concern is particularly strong in the field of software engineering, where AI can automate coding tasks and optimize processes. The media often amplifies these fears, painting a picture of a future where robots and intelligent machines replace human workers entirely.

Purpose of the Book

This book, "Why AI Will Not Eliminate Software Engineering Jobs," aims to dispel these fears and provide a balanced perspective. While it's true that AI will change the landscape of software engineering, it won't make human engineers redundant. Instead, AI will serve as a powerful tool that enhances human capabilities, allowing software engineers to focus on more complex and creative aspects of their work.

The Unique Value of Human Software Engineers

Software engineering is much more than just writing code. It involves creativity, problem-solving, and understanding user needs—areas where human engineers excel. AI can handle repetitive and data-intensive tasks, but it lacks the nuanced thinking and emotional intelligence that humans bring to the table. This book will explore how these human qualities are irreplaceable and essential for the success of software projects.

Overview of the Book

Throughout this book, we will delve into the strengths and limitations of AI, the critical role of human software engineers, and the symbiotic relationship between AI and humans in the field. We will look at real-world examples where AI and human engineers collaborate effectively and discuss the evolving role of software engineers in an AI-augmented world. By the end of this book, you will have a clear understanding of why AI will not eliminate software engineering jobs and how you can leverage AI to enhance your career.

Building Confidence for the Future

It's natural to feel apprehensive about the future, especially with the rapid pace of technological change. However, this book is here to reassure you. By embracing AI as a tool and continuously developing your skills, you can remain relevant and competitive in the job market. Remember, the human touch is invaluable, and your unique abilities as a software engineer will always be in demand.

Final Thoughts

As we embark on this journey, keep an open mind and be ready to see AI not as a threat but as an ally. Together, we'll explore the exciting possibilities that lie ahead and how you can thrive in a world where AI and human ingenuity work hand in hand.

By Mohammad Zaripour

Chapter 1

Chapter 1

Understanding AI and Its Capabilities

Introduction

Artificial Intelligence (AI) is no longer just a futuristic concept confined to sci-fi movies. Today, it's a powerful and rapidly evolving technology transforming various industries, including software engineering. As we dive into this topic, it's crucial to explore what AI truly is, its impressive capabilities, and the significant limitations that highlight the irreplaceable role of human software engineers.

What is AI?

Imagine having a tireless assistant who never gets bored, can sift through mountains of data in seconds, and learn from every interaction to improve its performance. That's AI in a nutshell. At its core, AI involves machines simulating human intelligence processes—learning, reasoning, and self-correction. AI encompasses various technologies like machine learning, where computers use algorithms to learn from data and make predictions, and deep learning, which involves neural networks with many layers to analyze data deeply.

Strengths of AI

AI's strengths are nothing short of remarkable:

- **Data Processing Power**: AI can process and analyze vast amounts of data faster and more accurately than any human. For instance, in healthcare, AI can analyze medical images to detect anomalies, often with higher precision than doctors. This capability is transforming industries that rely heavily on data, from finance to marketing.

- **Pattern Recognition**: AI is excellent at identifying patterns and making predictions. In finance, AI detects fraudulent transactions by spotting unusual patterns in spending behavior. In customer service, AI chatbots can handle routine inquiries with high accuracy, allowing human agents to focus on more complex issues.

- **Automation of Repetitive Tasks**: AI can automate mundane and repetitive tasks, freeing up human workers for more strategic and creative work. Think of AI as the ultimate assistant that handles the grunt work, so you don't have to.

Limitations of AI

Despite its strengths, AI has significant limitations that underscore the importance of human intelligence:

- **Lack of Creativity**: AI can analyze data and identify patterns, but it can't generate truly creative ideas or solutions. Creativity involves thinking outside the box and making unique connections—areas where humans excel.

- **Context Understanding**: AI often struggles with understanding context and nuance. It can process and analyze data but might miss subtle cues and deeper meanings that humans naturally grasp. In software engineering, understanding user needs and project requirements is crucial, and AI simply doesn't have the capability to fully understand these nuances.

- **Ethical and Moral Decision-Making**: AI lacks the ability to make ethical and moral decisions. While it can follow rules and guidelines, it doesn't possess the human qualities of empathy, compassion, and ethical reasoning necessary for decisions impacting people's lives.

AI and Software Engineering: A Symbiotic Relationship

In software engineering, AI is a powerful ally, not a replacement. AI can automate certain coding tasks, debug software, and optimize processes, but it cannot design complex systems, understand user requirements, or innovate in the way humans can.

For instance, AI can handle tasks like code generation, testing, and bug fixing, which saves time and reduces errors. This automation allows software engineers to focus on more strategic and creative aspects of their work. By leveraging AI tools, software engineers can increase their productivity and efficiency, leading to better software and faster development cycles.

Personal Stories and Case Studies

Consider Sarah, a software engineer at a leading tech firm. Sarah used AI tools to automate routine testing and bug-fixing tasks. This automation saved her countless hours, allowing her to focus on designing innovative features for her company's flagship product. The result? A more robust and user-friendly product that hit the market faster than anticipated.

Expanding Perspectives and Counterarguments

While many experts are optimistic about AI's potential, some caution against over-reliance on AI. Critics argue that AI's limitations, particularly in understanding context and making ethical decisions, pose significant risks. For instance, AI-driven decisions in hiring or law enforcement could perpetuate biases present in the training data, leading to unfair outcomes. Addressing these concerns is crucial for a balanced view of AI's role in software engineering.

Collaboration Between AI and Human Engineers: Unlocking Unprecedented Innovations

The synergy between AI and human engineers has the potential to revolutionize the field of software engineering, creating innovations that neither could achieve alone. This collaboration leverages the unique strengths of both AI and human intellect, fostering advancements that drive efficiency, creativity, and problem-solving to new heights.

Enhancing Problem-Solving Capabilities

One of the most significant benefits of combining AI with human engineers is the enhancement of problem-solving capabilities. AI systems excel at processing vast amounts of data quickly and accurately, identifying patterns and insights that might be missed by humans. When human engineers interpret these insights, they can apply their contextual knowledge and creativity to develop innovative solutions. For example, in software debugging, AI can quickly identify anomalies and potential errors, while human engineers can understand the broader context and implement nuanced fixes that improve overall system performance.

Accelerating Development Processes

AI tools can significantly accelerate the development process by automating repetitive and time-consuming tasks. Code generation, testing, and optimization can be performed by AI systems, freeing human engineers to focus on more complex and creative aspects of development. This collaboration not only speeds up the development cycle but also improves the quality of the software by reducing human errors. Additionally, AI-driven predictive analytics can help in anticipating potential issues before they become critical, allowing engineers to proactively address them.

Fostering Creativity and Innovation

AI can inspire human engineers to think outside the box by presenting novel ideas and solutions derived from analyzing large datasets. For instance, AI algorithms can suggest new design patterns or architectural frameworks that might not be immediately apparent to human engineers. This can lead to the development of groundbreaking applications and systems. Moreover, the ability of AI to simulate various scenarios and predict outcomes allows engineers to experiment with different approaches and iterate rapidly, fostering a culture of innovation and creativity.

Personalized Learning and Skill Development

AI-driven learning platforms can provide personalized training and development opportunities for engineers. By analyzing an engineer's strengths and weaknesses, AI can recommend targeted learning resources, practice exercises, and projects that help them improve their skills. This tailored approach ensures that engineers are continuously learning and adapting to new technologies and methodologies, keeping their skills relevant and cutting-edge.

Enhancing Collaboration and Communication

AI can facilitate better collaboration and communication among engineering teams. Natural language processing (NLP) tools can help in summarizing complex technical documents, translating technical jargon into understandable language for non-technical stakeholders, and even automating meeting summaries and action items. AI-powered project management tools can optimize task allocation, track progress, and predict potential roadblocks, enabling more efficient teamwork and coordination.

Pioneering New Frontiers

The collaboration between AI and human engineers opens the door to pioneering new frontiers in technology. For instance, in the field of artificial general intelligence (AGI), human engineers' creativity and understanding of human cognition are essential in guiding AI research and development. Similarly, in areas like quantum computing, biotechnology, and space exploration, the combined efforts of AI and human engineers are crucial for pushing the boundaries of what is possible and achieving breakthroughs that were previously unimaginable.

The collaboration between AI and human engineers is a powerful catalyst for innovation in software engineering. By leveraging the strengths of both AI and human intellect, we can enhance problem-solving capabilities, accelerate development processes, foster creativity, and pioneer new technological frontiers. This symbiotic relationship not only leads to more efficient and effective engineering practices but also drives the development of groundbreaking solutions that have the potential to transform industries and improve lives. As we continue to explore and refine this collaboration, the possibilities for innovation are boundless, promising a future where AI and human engineers work together to achieve extraordinary advancements.

Ensuring Ethical Use of AI in Software Engineering: Mitigating Bias and Inequality

As AI technologies continue to advance and integrate into various aspects of software engineering, ensuring their ethical use has become a critical responsibility for software engineers. The potential for AI to perpetuate biases and inequalities is significant, given that AI systems are often trained on historical data that may reflect societal prejudices. This section explores strategies and best practices that software engineers can adopt to ensure AI tools are used ethically and do not perpetuate biases or inequalities.

Understanding the Ethical Implications of AI

To begin with, it is crucial for engineers to remain informed about the latest developments in AI ethics. This involves participating in workshops, attending conferences, and taking courses focused on ethical AI. Incorporating ethics training into professional development programs is also essential. Understanding the ethical implications of AI helps engineers recognize and address potential issues early in the development process.

Using tools and frameworks designed to detect biases in AI models is another important step. Tools like IBM's AI Fairness 360 and Google's What-If Tool can help identify and visualize bias in datasets and models. Ensuring that training datasets are representative and diverse reduces the risk of perpetuating existing biases and helps create more equitable AI systems. Conducting regular bias audits of AI systems, preferably by independent third parties, can provide an objective assessment of an AI system's fairness.

Incorporating Ethical Practices in AI Development

Transparent development processes are key to ethical AI use. Maintaining detailed documentation of AI development processes, including data sources, model selection, and evaluation metrics, helps stakeholders understand the decision-making process and fosters trust. Developing AI models that are interpretable and explainable is also crucial, as users need to understand how decisions are made by AI systems to ensure accountability.

Fostering diversity within development teams can help identify potential ethical issues that may not be apparent to a homogenous group. Engaging with a broad range of stakeholders, including those who may be affected by AI systems, ensures that diverse viewpoints are considered in the development process.

Implementing Governance and Accountability

Adopting established ethical frameworks and guidelines, such as the IEEE's Ethically Aligned Design or the EU's Guidelines for Trustworthy AI, provides a structured approach to ethical AI development. Creating and enforcing internal policies that prioritize ethical AI development, setting clear expectations for ethical conduct, and establishing mechanisms for reporting and addressing ethical concerns are also important steps.

Establishing ethics committees or boards within organizations to oversee AI projects is essential. These committees should include ethicists, legal experts, and diverse representatives to provide comprehensive oversight. Conducting regular impact assessments to evaluate the societal and ethical implications of AI systems, considering the potential for harm, and identifying strategies for mitigation are necessary practices.

Promoting Ethical AI in the Broader Community

Collaborating with other organizations and industry groups to promote ethical AI standards can drive collective action toward ethical AI. Participation in initiatives like the Partnership on AI can help in this endeavor. Advocating for ethical AI through public speaking, writing, and community engagement raises awareness about the importance of ethical AI and helps build public trust.

Keeping abreast of regulatory developments related to AI ensures compliance with laws and regulations, adhering to legal and ethical standards. Proactively engaging with regulators and policymakers to help shape the development of ethical AI regulations is also crucial. Engineers can provide valuable insights into the technical and ethical challenges of AI.

Ensuring the ethical use of AI tools in software engineering is a multifaceted challenge that requires a combination of awareness, education, inclusive design, transparent processes, governance, and advocacy. By adopting these strategies, software engineers can mitigate biases, promote fairness, and ensure that AI technologies contribute positively to society. The commitment to ethical AI development is not just a professional obligation but also a societal imperative, ensuring that AI advancements benefit all members of society equitably.

Visuals and Analogies

Imagine AI as a super-powered magnifying glass. It can zoom in on tiny details within massive datasets, revealing patterns and insights invisible to the naked eye. This ability is akin to having a superhuman assistant who tirelessly combs through data to find the nuggets of gold that drive innovation.

Strategies for Software Engineers to Stay Relevant in an AI-Augmented Job Market

As the integration of AI into the job market continues to evolve, software engineers must adopt proactive strategies to remain relevant and competitive. The rapid pace of technological advancements necessitates a commitment to continuous learning and adaptability. Here are several strategies that software engineers can employ to thrive in an AI-augmented job market.

Continuous Learning and Skill Development

1. **Lifelong Learning Mindset**

    o Embrace a lifelong learning mindset. Stay curious and open to acquiring new knowledge and skills. This includes staying updated with the latest advancements in AI and other emerging technologies.

    o Enroll in online courses, attend workshops, and participate in webinars to keep abreast of new developments. Platforms like

Coursera, Udacity, and edX offer courses on AI, machine learning, and related topics.

2. **Certifications and Advanced Degrees**

    o Pursue relevant certifications and advanced degrees to deepen your expertise. Certifications from recognized institutions, such as AI certifications from Google or Microsoft, can enhance your credentials and demonstrate your commitment to staying current.

    o Consider advanced degrees in AI, data science, or related fields to gain in-depth knowledge and a competitive edge in the job market.

3. **Skill Diversification**

    o Diversify your skill set by learning interdisciplinary skills that complement software engineering. This includes understanding data science, cybersecurity, cloud computing, and user experience (UX) design.

- Acquiring knowledge in these areas can make you a more versatile and valuable asset to employers.

Hands-On Experience and Practical Application

4. **Projects and Practical Experience**

    - Engage in hands-on projects that apply AI and machine learning techniques. Practical experience helps reinforce theoretical knowledge and demonstrates your ability to implement AI solutions in real-world scenarios.

    - Contribute to open-source projects or start your own projects to build a portfolio that showcases your skills and experience.

5. **Internships and Collaborations**

- Seek internships, co-op opportunities, or collaborations with companies working on cutting-edge AI technologies. Real-world experience is invaluable in understanding industry applications and gaining practical insights.

- Collaborate with peers or join tech communities and hackathons to work on innovative projects and expand your network.

Networking and Community Engagement

6. Professional Networks

- Build and maintain a strong professional network. Attend industry conferences, meetups, and networking events to connect with other professionals and stay informed about industry trends.

- Join professional organizations such as the IEEE, ACM, or local tech groups to access resources, attend events, and participate in discussions.

7. **Mentorship and Knowledge Sharing**

    o Seek mentorship from experienced professionals in the AI and software engineering fields. Mentors can provide guidance, share industry insights, and help you navigate your career path.

    o Actively participate in knowledge-sharing activities, such as writing blogs, giving talks, or contributing to forums. Sharing your knowledge not only helps others but also reinforces your understanding and builds your reputation.

Adaptability and Forward-Thinking

8. **Stay Informed About Industry Trends**

    o Keep a close eye on industry trends and technological advancements. Read industry publications, follow influential thought leaders on social media, and subscribe to newsletters and podcasts.

- Understanding where the industry is headed allows you to anticipate changes and prepare accordingly.

9. **Embrace Change and Innovation**

    - Be open to change and willing to adapt to new technologies and methodologies. Embracing innovation and being flexible in your approach will enable you to stay relevant as the job market evolves.

    - Experiment with new tools and frameworks, and be willing to pivot your career focus as needed to align with emerging opportunities.

Ethical and Responsible AI Development

10. **Ethical AI Practices**

- Develop a strong understanding of ethical AI practices and commit to building responsible AI systems. Ethical considerations are increasingly important in the tech industry, and being knowledgeable in this area can set you apart.

- Stay informed about regulations and best practices related to AI ethics, privacy, and security. Contributing to the development of ethical guidelines and advocating for responsible AI use demonstrates your commitment to the field.

Staying relevant in an AI-augmented job market requires a multifaceted approach that combines continuous learning, practical experience, networking, adaptability, and a commitment to ethical practices. By embracing these strategies, software engineers can not only maintain their relevance but also thrive in an ever-evolving technological landscape. The key is to remain proactive, curious, and open to new opportunities, ensuring that you are always prepared to meet the demands of the future.

By Mohammad Zaripour

The Human Advantage: Why Software Engineers Will Thrive Alongside AI

While AI offers numerous benefits, such as automating repetitive tasks, enhancing data analysis, and improving efficiency, it cannot replace the unique qualities that human software engineers bring to the table. AI excels in processing large amounts of data quickly and accurately, but it lacks the creativity, emotional intelligence, and nuanced problem-solving abilities that humans possess.

Human engineers are adept at understanding user needs, designing intuitive interfaces, and developing innovative solutions that address complex challenges. These skills are essential for creating software that is not only functional but also user-friendly and engaging. Moreover, engineers bring empathy and ethical judgment to their work, ensuring that AI applications are developed and used responsibly.

As AI continues to evolve, it will serve as a powerful tool that enhances the capabilities of software engineers rather than replacing them. By automating routine tasks, AI allows engineers to focus on higher-level strategic planning, system design, and innovation. This shift enables engineers to tackle more complex problems and drive technological advancements.

The integration of AI into software development creates new opportunities for engineers to specialize in areas such as AI and machine learning, further expanding their career prospects. By embracing AI as a partner and continuously developing their skills, software engineers can remain relevant and competitive in the job market.

In conclusion, while AI brings significant benefits to the field of software engineering, it is the unique human qualities of creativity, empathy, and ethical judgment that ensure software engineers will continue to thrive. AI and human engineers working together will lead to greater innovation and a more dynamic and fulfilling profession.

Staying Ahead: Essential Workshops, Courses, and Certifications for Software Engineers

To keep their knowledge up-to-date and remain competitive in an AI-driven market, software engineers should actively pursue continuous learning through various workshops, training courses, and certifications. Here are some specific recommendations:

Workshops and Training Courses:

1. **Coursera: Machine Learning by Andrew Ng** - This popular course provides a comprehensive introduction to machine learning, covering key concepts and practical applications. It is ideal for engineers looking to understand the fundamentals of AI.

2. **Udacity: AI for Everyone by Andrew Ng** - This course is designed to help engineers and non-engineers alike understand AI technologies and their implications. It covers the basics of AI, machine learning, and deep learning.

3. **edX: Professional Certificate in Computer Science for Artificial Intelligence by Harvard University** - This program includes courses on AI, machine learning, and data science, providing a solid foundation for engineers looking to specialize in AI.

4. **MIT OpenCourseWare: Artificial Intelligence** - MIT offers free online courses that cover various aspects of AI, including algorithms, neural networks, and robotics. These courses are excellent for engineers seeking in-depth knowledge.

5. **Kaggle: Data Science and Machine Learning Competitions** - Participating in Kaggle competitions allows engineers to apply their skills to real-world problems, gain hands-on experience, and learn from a community of data scientists and AI experts.

Certifications:

1. **Google Professional Machine Learning Engineer** - This certification validates an engineer's ability to design, build, and productionize machine learning models. It covers topics such as data engineering, machine learning modeling, and deployment.

2. **Microsoft Certified: Azure AI Engineer Associate** - This certification focuses on using Azure AI services to build and deploy AI solutions. It is ideal for engineers working with Microsoft's cloud platform.

3. **IBM AI Engineering Professional Certificate** - Offered through Coursera, this certification covers machine learning, deep learning, and AI applications. It

includes hands-on projects and practical experience with IBM's AI tools.

4. **AWS Certified Machine Learning – Specialty** - This certification is designed for engineers who want to demonstrate their expertise in building, training, and deploying machine learning models on the AWS platform.

5. **Certified Artificial Intelligence Practitioner (CAIP)** - Offered by the CertNexus, this certification provides a comprehensive understanding of AI concepts, techniques, and applications. It is suitable for engineers looking to validate their AI skills.

By participating in these workshops, training courses, and obtaining relevant certifications, software engineers can stay ahead of the curve and ensure their skills remain current in an AI-driven market. Continuous learning and professional development are key to thriving in the evolving field of software engineering.

Reflection Questions

How do you think AI can enhance your current job responsibilities?

By Mohammad Zaripour

Artificial Intelligence (AI) has the potential to significantly enhance job responsibilities in various ways. One of the primary benefits is the automation of repetitive tasks. Many jobs involve routine activities that can be time-consuming and monotonous. AI can take over these tasks, allowing employees to focus on more complex and creative aspects of their work. For instance, in data entry roles, AI can quickly and accurately input data, reducing the chances of human error and freeing up time for employees to analyze and interpret the data.

Another way AI can enhance job responsibilities is through improved decision-making. AI systems can process vast amounts of information much faster than humans. They can analyze data, identify patterns, and provide insights that might not be immediately apparent to a human. This can be particularly useful in fields like finance, healthcare, and marketing, where making informed decisions quickly is crucial. For example, in healthcare, AI can help doctors diagnose diseases more accurately by analyzing medical records and imaging data.

AI can also enhance communication and collaboration within teams. Tools powered by AI, such as chatbots and virtual assistants, can facilitate better communication by providing instant responses to queries and managing schedules. These tools can help ensure that team members are always on the same page, reducing misunderstandings and improving overall productivity. In customer service roles, AI chatbots can handle common inquiries, allowing human agents to focus on more complex customer issues.

Personalization is another area where AI can make a significant impact. In marketing and sales, AI can analyze customer data to provide personalized recommendations and offers. This not only improves the customer experience but also increases the chances of successful sales. Similarly, in education, AI can tailor learning experiences to individual students' needs, helping them to learn more effectively.

AI can also assist in professional development. AI-driven platforms can recommend training programs and resources based on an individual's career goals and current skill set. This can help employees stay up-to-date with industry trends and continuously improve their skills. For example, an AI system might suggest courses on the latest software tools for a graphic designer, helping them to remain competitive in their field.

In summary, AI has the potential to transform job responsibilities by automating routine tasks, enhancing decision-making, improving communication and collaboration, personalizing experiences, and supporting professional development. By leveraging AI, employees can work more efficiently and effectively, ultimately leading to greater job satisfaction and productivity.

What unique qualities do you bring to your role that AI cannot replicate?

Humans possess a range of unique qualities that are difficult, if not impossible, for AI to replicate. One of the most significant of these is emotional intelligence. Emotional intelligence involves the ability to understand, manage, and express one's own emotions, as well as to recognize and influence the emotions of others. This skill is crucial in many roles, particularly those that involve teamwork, leadership, and customer interaction. For example, a manager who can empathize with their team members and provide support during challenging times can foster a positive work environment and motivate their team more effectively than an AI system.

Another unique quality is creativity. While AI can generate content based on patterns and data, it lacks the ability to think outside the box and come up with truly original ideas. Creativity involves not just the generation of new ideas, but also the ability to connect seemingly unrelated concepts in innovative ways. This is essential in fields such as marketing, design, and research, where novel solutions and fresh perspectives are highly valued. A human designer, for instance, can draw inspiration from personal experiences and cultural contexts to create unique and compelling designs.

Humans also bring a deep understanding of context and nuance to their roles. This includes the ability to interpret and respond to complex social cues, cultural references, and situational subtleties. AI, on the other hand, often struggles with these aspects, as it relies on predefined rules and data sets. In customer service, for example, a human agent can pick up on a customer's tone of voice or body language to provide a more personalized and empathetic response, something that AI chatbots may find challenging.

Ethical judgment is another area where humans excel. Making ethical decisions often requires considering a wide range of factors, including moral principles, societal norms, and potential consequences. While AI can be programmed with ethical guidelines, it lacks the ability to fully understand and weigh these factors in the same way a human can. This is particularly important in fields such as law, healthcare, and education, where ethical considerations are paramount. A doctor, for example, must balance the potential benefits and risks of a treatment plan, taking into account the patient's unique circumstances and values.

Adaptability is a further strength of humans. People can quickly adjust to new situations, learn from their experiences, and apply their knowledge in different contexts. This flexibility is crucial in a rapidly changing world, where new challenges and opportunities constantly arise. AI systems, in contrast, often require extensive reprogramming and data updates to adapt to new conditions. A human employee can swiftly pivot their approach in response to unexpected developments, ensuring that their organization remains agile and resilient.

In summary, while AI offers many advantages, it cannot replicate the emotional intelligence, creativity, contextual understanding, ethical judgment, and adaptability that humans bring to their roles. These qualities enable humans to navigate complex social interactions, generate innovative ideas, make nuanced decisions, and adapt to changing circumstances, making them indispensable in the modern workplace.

Chapter summary:

Understanding the capabilities and limitations of AI is crucial for appreciating its role in the future of software engineering. While AI can significantly enhance productivity and efficiency, it cannot replace the unique qualities that human software engineers bring to the profession. By recognizing the strengths of both AI and human engineers, we can create a collaborative environment where technology and human ingenuity work together to achieve remarkable results.

Chapter 2

Chapter 2

The Human Element in Software Engineering

Introduction

In a world where AI is making waves across various industries, it's easy to overlook the indispensable role of human creativity, intuition, and emotional intelligence in software engineering. While AI can handle repetitive tasks and analyze vast amounts of data, it is the human element that drives innovation, empathizes with users, and ultimately shapes the future of technology. This chapter delves into the unique strengths that human software engineers bring to the table, highlighting why they remain irreplaceable in the age of AI.

Creativity and Innovation

AI excels at pattern recognition and data processing but lacks the ability to think creatively or innovate. Creativity involves imagining new possibilities, making unexpected connections, and thinking outside the box—skills that are inherently human.

Consider the development of groundbreaking technologies like the World Wide Web, the smartphone, or revolutionary software like Photoshop. These innovations didn't arise from algorithms or data patterns; they were the result of human imagination and the relentless pursuit of new ideas. Human software engineers continuously push the boundaries of what's possible, envisioning and creating technologies that AI could never conceive on its own.

Emotional Intelligence and User Empathy

Understanding user needs and designing software that meets those needs is a deeply human endeavor. Emotional intelligence allows software engineers to empathize with users, understanding their pain points, desires, and behaviors. This empathy translates into user-friendly interfaces, intuitive designs, and solutions that resonate with people on a personal level.

For instance, consider the development of a mental health app designed to provide support and resources for individuals struggling with anxiety and depression. While AI can analyze user data and suggest interventions, it takes a human touch to design the app in a way that feels comforting, safe, and genuinely supportive. Human software engineers can create experiences that are not only functional but also emotionally resonant.

Collaboration and Team Dynamics

Software development is rarely a solo endeavor. It involves collaboration among teams of designers, developers, testers, and stakeholders. Human engineers bring communication skills, the ability to work well with others, and the capacity to navigate the complexities of team dynamics.

Effective collaboration often leads to innovative solutions as team members bounce ideas off one another, offer diverse perspectives, and collectively problem-solve. AI might assist in project management or provide technical insights, but it cannot replicate the nuanced interactions and relationships that drive successful teamwork.

Ethical Decision-Making

Ethical considerations are integral to software development, especially as technology becomes more pervasive in our daily lives. Human software engineers are equipped to make ethical decisions, weighing the potential impacts of their work on society. They can consider questions of privacy, fairness, and the long-term consequences of technological advancements.

For example, developing AI-driven facial recognition software raises significant ethical concerns regarding privacy and potential misuse. Human engineers can navigate these ethical dilemmas, ensuring that technology serves the greater good and respects individual rights.

Personal Stories and Case Studies

Take the story of Alex, a software engineer working on a social networking platform. When developing a new feature designed to suggest friends, Alex realized that the algorithm might inadvertently reinforce social bubbles, limiting users' exposure to diverse viewpoints. By recognizing this potential issue, Alex worked with the team to adjust the feature, ensuring it promoted diverse interactions. This example highlights the importance of human insight and ethical considerations in software development.

Quotes and References

As renowned AI researcher Fei-Fei Li aptly put it, "AI is everywhere. It's not that big, scary thing in the future. AI is here with us." This quote underscores the pervasive presence of AI while reminding us that human oversight and creativity are crucial in guiding its application.

Integrating Human Creativity and Empathy into AI-Driven Software Development

As AI-driven software development becomes increasingly prevalent, integrating unique human qualities such as creativity and empathy into these processes is essential. These human attributes can enhance the functionality and user experience of AI systems, leading to more innovative, user-friendly, and ethically sound software solutions. Here's how software engineers can effectively incorporate creativity and empathy into AI-driven development.

Emphasizing Creativity in AI Development

1. **Collaborative Ideation**

    o Encourage collaborative brainstorming sessions where human engineers and AI tools work together. AI can generate a wide range of possibilities based on existing data, while human engineers can sift through these ideas, combining and refining them into novel solutions.

- Use AI to explore unconventional design patterns and algorithms, pushing the boundaries of traditional software engineering. This partnership can lead to groundbreaking innovations that purely human or purely AI-driven efforts might not achieve.

2. **Creative Problem-Solving**

    - Leverage AI's ability to analyze large datasets and identify patterns to provide creative insights into complex problems. Human engineers can interpret these insights, applying their domain knowledge and creative thinking to develop unique solutions.

    - Implement AI tools that assist in rapid prototyping, allowing engineers to experiment with different ideas quickly. This iterative process encourages creativity and innovation.

3. **Artistic Integration**

    o Incorporate elements of art and design into AI development processes. Engage designers, artists, and other creative professionals to work alongside engineers, ensuring that the software is not only functional but also aesthetically pleasing and engaging.

    o Use AI to create and suggest artistic elements, such as UI/UX designs, color schemes, and visual effects, which human engineers can refine and adapt based on their creative vision.

Incorporating Empathy in AI-Driven Development

4. **User-Centered Design**

    o Implement user-centered design principles, ensuring that the development process begins and ends with the user's needs and experiences. Conduct user research, interviews, and surveys to gather insights into the target audience's preferences, pain points, and expectations.

- Use AI to analyze user feedback and behavior patterns, identifying trends and areas for improvement. Human engineers can interpret this data with empathy, understanding the context and emotions behind user interactions, leading to more intuitive and user-friendly designs.

5. **Ethical Considerations**

    - Integrate ethical considerations into the AI development process. Develop AI systems that respect user privacy, promote fairness, and avoid biases. Human empathy is crucial in identifying potential ethical issues and ensuring that AI solutions are developed responsibly.

    - Establish ethics committees and involve diverse stakeholders in the development process to provide different perspectives and ensure that the software addresses a broad range of ethical concerns.

6. **Emotionally Intelligent AI**

    o Design AI systems that can recognize and respond to human emotions. This involves training AI models on diverse datasets that include emotional cues and contexts. Human engineers can guide the development of these models, ensuring that the AI's responses are appropriate and empathetic.

    o Develop AI interfaces that are capable of expressing empathy through natural language processing (NLP) and sentiment analysis. For example, customer service chatbots can be programmed to recognize frustration or confusion in users' messages and respond with understanding and support.

Blending Creativity and Empathy

7. **Interdisciplinary Teams**

    o Form interdisciplinary teams that bring together engineers, designers, psychologists, and other experts to collaborate on AI projects. This diversity of perspectives fosters a development environment where creativity and empathy are naturally integrated.

- o Encourage cross-functional collaboration and open communication within teams, creating a culture that values both technical excellence and human-centered design.

8. **Continuous Feedback and Iteration**

- o Establish a feedback loop that involves continuous user testing and iteration. By regularly soliciting and analyzing user feedback, engineers can ensure that the software evolves in response to users' needs and emotions.

- o Use AI to gather and process user feedback efficiently, but rely on human empathy to interpret and act on this feedback, making adjustments that enhance the user experience.

9. **Storytelling and Narratives**

- Use storytelling techniques to humanize AI systems. Create narratives that explain how the AI works, why certain features were developed, and how they benefit the user. This approach helps users connect emotionally with the technology.

- Develop AI-driven applications that incorporate storytelling elements, such as personalized recommendations or interactive experiences that resonate with users on an emotional level.

Integrating human creativity and empathy into AI-driven software development processes enhances the innovation, usability, and ethical integrity of the resulting solutions. By fostering a collaborative environment that values these human qualities, engineers can create AI systems that not only perform complex tasks efficiently but also connect with users on a deeper level. This synergy between AI and human attributes ultimately leads to more meaningful and impactful technological advancements.

Potential Risks of Over-Reliance on AI in Software Engineering and Mitigation Strategies

While AI offers numerous advantages in software engineering, an over-reliance on AI can introduce significant risks. These risks can impact the quality, security, and ethical standards of software development. It is crucial to identify these risks and implement strategies to mitigate them, ensuring a balanced and responsible approach to AI integration in software engineering.

Risks of Over-Reliance on AI

1. **Loss of Human Expertise**

    - **Risk**: As AI automates more tasks, there is a risk that software engineers may lose critical skills and expertise. Over time, the dependency on AI tools could lead to a decline in the depth of human knowledge and the ability to solve complex problems without AI assistance.

    - **Mitigation**: Encourage continuous learning and professional development for engineers. Implement training programs that focus on both AI and traditional software engineering skills, ensuring that human expertise remains robust.

2. **Bias and Fairness Issues**

    o **Risk**: AI systems can inadvertently perpetuate biases present in the training data. If these biases are not identified and addressed, they can lead to unfair and discriminatory outcomes in software applications.

    o **Mitigation**: Implement rigorous testing and validation processes to detect and mitigate biases in AI models. Use diverse and representative datasets for training AI systems and involve multidisciplinary teams to review and address potential biases.

3. **Security Vulnerabilities**

    o **Risk**: AI systems, like any software, can be vulnerable to attacks. Over-reliance on AI can lead to complacency, where security measures are not adequately implemented or reviewed by human experts.

    o **Mitigation**: Incorporate robust security practices in the development and deployment of AI systems. Conduct regular security audits, and involve security experts to identify and address potential vulnerabilities.

4. **Transparency and Accountability**

   o **Risk**: AI systems, especially those that use complex algorithms, can act as "black boxes," making it difficult to understand their decision-making processes. This lack of transparency can hinder accountability and trust.

   o **Mitigation**: Develop and implement explainable AI (XAI) techniques that make AI decision-making processes more transparent. Ensure that there are clear accountability frameworks for the development and deployment of AI systems.

5. **Overfitting and Generalization Issues**

   o **Risk**: AI models trained on specific datasets may overfit, performing well on the training data but poorly in real-world scenarios. This can result in software that is unreliable and unable to generalize effectively.

- **Mitigation**: Use cross-validation and diverse datasets to train AI models, ensuring they generalize well to different contexts. Continuously monitor and update AI systems to maintain their performance over time.

6. **Ethical and Moral Considerations**

    - **Risk**: AI systems may make decisions that are ethically or morally questionable, especially in scenarios where human judgment is crucial. Over-reliance on AI could lead to outcomes that conflict with societal values.

    - **Mitigation**: Establish ethical guidelines and review processes for AI development. Involve ethicists and other stakeholders in the design and deployment of AI systems to ensure that they align with ethical standards.

7. **Job Displacement and Economic Impact**

    o **Risk**: Automation through AI can lead to job displacement, causing economic and social disruption. This can particularly affect roles that are heavily dependent on repetitive tasks.

    o **Mitigation**: Develop strategies for workforce transition, including retraining programs and career development initiatives. Promote the creation of new job roles that complement AI, focusing on areas where human skills are irreplaceable.

8. **Over-Dependence on AI Vendors**

    o **Risk**: Relying too heavily on third-party AI tools and vendors can create dependencies that are difficult to manage. This can lead to issues with vendor lock-in, data privacy, and control over the AI systems.

    o **Mitigation**: Diversify AI tools and vendors to avoid dependency on a single source. Consider developing in-house AI capabilities where feasible, and ensure that data privacy and control measures are in place.

While AI can significantly enhance software engineering, it is crucial to recognize and mitigate the risks associated with over-reliance on AI. By maintaining a balance between AI and human expertise, addressing biases, ensuring transparency and security, and considering ethical implications, software engineers can leverage AI responsibly and effectively. This balanced approach will help maximize the benefits of AI while minimizing potential drawbacks, leading to more reliable, ethical, and innovative software solutions.

Reflection Questions

How have you leveraged your creativity and empathy in your software engineering projects?

Creativity and empathy play crucial roles in software engineering, often leading to more innovative and user-friendly solutions. Here's how I've leveraged these qualities in my projects:

Creativity in software engineering involves thinking beyond conventional solutions and exploring new ways to solve problems. For instance, in a recent project, I was tasked with developing a feature for a mobile app that would enhance user engagement. Instead of following the standard approach, I brainstormed various interactive elements and gamification techniques. By incorporating a rewards system and personalized challenges, I was able to create a more engaging and enjoyable user experience. This creative approach not only met the project requirements but also exceeded user expectations, resulting in higher user retention rates.

Empathy, on the other hand, involves understanding and addressing the needs and emotions of users. In another project, I was working on a healthcare application designed for elderly users. Recognizing that this demographic might not be as tech-savvy, I focused on creating an intuitive and accessible interface. I conducted user interviews and usability tests with elderly participants to gather feedback and understand their pain points. This empathetic approach allowed me to design features that were easy to navigate, with larger buttons and clear instructions, ultimately making the app more user-friendly for its intended audience.

Combining creativity and empathy, I also worked on a project aimed at improving mental health through a digital platform. Understanding the sensitive nature of mental health, I designed the platform to be both supportive and engaging. I incorporated features such as mood tracking, personalized content, and virtual support groups. By empathizing with users' needs and creatively addressing them, I was able to develop a platform that provided meaningful support and fostered a sense of community among users.

In summary, leveraging creativity and empathy in software engineering projects leads to innovative solutions that truly resonate with users. By thinking outside the box and understanding the user's perspective, I've been able to create applications that are not only functional but also engaging and user-friendly. These qualities ensure that the software meets the needs of its users and provides a positive experience, ultimately contributing to the success of the project.

Can you think of a time when ethical considerations influenced your work?

Ethical considerations often play a crucial role in software engineering, guiding decisions to ensure that the technology we create is used responsibly and benefits society. One particular instance stands out in my experience.

I was working on a project that involved developing a data analytics platform for a client in the healthcare industry. The platform was designed to collect and analyze patient data to improve treatment outcomes. While the potential benefits were significant, there were also serious ethical concerns regarding patient privacy and data security.

From the outset, I knew that handling sensitive health information required stringent measures to protect patient confidentiality. I advocated for implementing robust encryption protocols and strict access controls to ensure that only authorized personnel could access the data. Additionally, I pushed for the inclusion of anonymization techniques to strip personally identifiable information from the data sets before analysis. This would help mitigate the risk of data breaches and unauthorized access.

Another ethical consideration was obtaining informed consent from patients. It was essential that patients were fully aware of how their data would be used and had the opportunity to opt out if they were uncomfortable. I worked closely with the client to develop clear and transparent consent forms, ensuring that patients understood their rights and the purpose of the data collection.

Throughout the project, I also emphasized the importance of regular security audits and compliance with relevant regulations, such as the

Health Insurance Portability and Accountability Act (HIPAA) in the United States. These measures were crucial in maintaining the trust of patients and ensuring that the platform adhered to the highest ethical standards.

In summary, ethical considerations significantly influenced my work on this project. By prioritizing patient privacy, informed consent, and data security, I was able to develop a platform that not only met the client's needs but also upheld the ethical standards essential in healthcare. This experience reinforced the importance of integrating ethical principles into every stage of software development, ensuring that technology serves the greater good.

Chapter summary:

While AI continues to advance and augment the field of software engineering, the human element remains irreplaceable. Creativity, emotional intelligence, collaboration, and ethical decision-making are all areas where human engineers excel and will continue to drive the industry forward. By embracing these unique strengths, software engineers can ensure that technology serves humanity in meaningful and positive ways.

Chapter 3

Chapter 3

AI and the Future of Software Engineering Jobs

Introduction

As AI technology continues to evolve, it's natural for software engineers to wonder how it might impact their careers. Will AI take over their jobs, or will it transform the nature of their work? This chapter explores the future of software engineering in the context of AI advancements. We'll examine how AI is reshaping the industry, the new opportunities it creates, and how engineers can adapt to stay relevant in this changing landscape.

By Mohammad Zaripour

AI's Impact on Software Engineering Roles

AI is already influencing software engineering in several significant ways. From automating repetitive tasks to enhancing development processes, AI is changing how engineers approach their work. Here's a look at some key areas where AI is making an impact:

- **Automation of Routine Tasks**: AI tools can automate mundane tasks such as code generation, bug detection, and testing. For example, AI-powered code editors can suggest improvements or flag errors in real-time, speeding up the development process and reducing human error. This automation allows engineers to focus on more complex and creative aspects of their work.

- **Enhanced Data Analysis**: AI can analyze large datasets quickly, providing valuable insights that help in making data-driven decisions. Engineers can use AI to understand user behavior, optimize software performance, and personalize user experiences based on data trends.

- **Improved Software Testing**: AI can enhance software testing by creating and executing test cases more efficiently.

Automated testing frameworks powered by AI can identify potential issues and vulnerabilities, ensuring that software is robust and reliable before it reaches the end-users.

Emerging Opportunities in Software Engineering

While AI may automate certain aspects of software development, it also creates new opportunities for engineers. Here's how:

- **Focus on Higher-Level Tasks**: With routine tasks automated, engineers can dedicate more time to strategic planning, system design, and innovation. This shift allows engineers to work on more complex projects, develop new technologies, and solve intricate problems that AI alone cannot address.

- **Collaboration with AI Tools**: Engineers will increasingly collaborate with AI tools to enhance their productivity and creativity. Understanding how to integrate AI into development workflows, customize AI solutions, and leverage AI insights will become essential skills.

- **AI and Machine Learning Specializations**: As AI technology advances, there will be growing demand for engineers with expertise in AI and machine learning. Specializing in these areas can open up new career paths, such as developing AI algorithms, creating intelligent systems, and designing AI-driven applications.

Skills for the Future

To thrive in an AI-driven future, software engineers should focus on developing skills that complement AI technology. Key skills include:

- **Creativity and Problem-Solving**: While AI can handle repetitive tasks, it cannot replace human creativity and problem-solving abilities. Engineers should cultivate their creativity and ability to think critically to tackle complex challenges and drive innovation.

- **Interdisciplinary Knowledge**: Understanding how AI intersects with various fields—such as data science, cybersecurity, and user experience—can provide a competitive edge. Engineers who can integrate AI with other technologies and domains will be well-positioned for future opportunities.

- **Adaptability and Continuous Learning**: The tech industry evolves rapidly, and engineers must be adaptable and committed to continuous learning. Staying updated with the latest AI developments, tools, and best practices will help engineers remain relevant and competitive.

Case Studies and Personal Stories

Consider the story of Priya, a software engineer who embraced AI in her work. Priya used AI-powered tools to streamline her development process, allowing her to focus on designing innovative features for her company's applications. By learning to integrate AI into her workflow, Priya not only enhanced her productivity but also positioned herself as a leader in her field.

Quotes and References

"AI is not a replacement for human work but a tool that augments human capabilities," says Sundar Pichai, CEO of Google. This quote highlights the complementary nature of AI and human skills, reinforcing that AI enhances rather than replaces human contributions.

Reflection Questions

How can software engineers balance the benefits of AI automation with the need to maintain their unique human skills, such as creativity and problem-solving, in their daily work?

Balancing the benefits of AI automation with the need to maintain unique human skills requires a strategic approach. Software engineers can start by identifying which tasks are best suited for automation and which require human ingenuity. Routine and repetitive tasks, such as code generation, bug detection, and basic testing, can be efficiently handled by AI tools. This allows engineers to allocate more time to tasks that demand creativity and complex problem-solving, such as designing innovative features, developing new algorithms, and addressing unique user needs.

To maintain and enhance their creative and problem-solving skills, engineers should actively seek opportunities for continuous learning and professional development. Engaging in activities such as brainstorming sessions, hackathons, and collaborative projects can stimulate creative thinking and provide fresh perspectives. Additionally, engineers can benefit from interdisciplinary learning, exploring fields like design thinking, psychology, and user experience to gain new insights and approaches to problem-solving.

By integrating AI tools into their workflow, engineers can enhance their productivity and efficiency while preserving the human touch that is essential for innovation. For example, using AI-powered code editors can streamline the coding process, allowing engineers to focus on higher-level design and architecture. Regularly reflecting on their work and seeking feedback from peers can also help engineers stay grounded in their unique skills and continuously improve their craft.

What ethical considerations should software engineers keep in mind when developing AI-driven applications, and how can they ensure that these applications are used responsibly?

When developing AI-driven applications, software engineers must prioritize ethical considerations to ensure that their creations are used responsibly and do not cause harm. One of the primary ethical concerns is data privacy. Engineers must implement robust data protection measures, such as encryption and anonymization, to safeguard user information and prevent unauthorized access. It is also essential to obtain informed consent from users, clearly explaining how their data will be used and giving them the option to opt out.

Another critical ethical consideration is bias in AI algorithms. Engineers must be vigilant in identifying and mitigating biases that may arise from training data or algorithm design. This involves using diverse and representative datasets, conducting thorough testing, and continuously monitoring AI systems for biased outcomes. Transparency is key; engineers should document their methodologies and be open about the limitations and potential biases of their AI models.

To ensure responsible use of AI applications, engineers should adhere to established ethical guidelines and industry standards. Engaging with interdisciplinary teams, including ethicists, legal experts, and social scientists, can provide valuable perspectives and help address complex ethical issues. Additionally, fostering a culture of ethical awareness within the organization and encouraging open discussions about ethical dilemmas can promote responsible AI development.

In what ways can software engineers leverage interdisciplinary knowledge to enhance their collaboration with AI tools and stay competitive in an evolving industry?

Leveraging interdisciplinary knowledge is crucial for software engineers to enhance their collaboration with AI tools and remain competitive in an evolving industry. By gaining insights from fields such as data science, cybersecurity, and user experience, engineers can develop a more holistic understanding of AI and its applications.

For instance, knowledge of data science can help engineers better understand the principles of machine learning and data analysis, enabling them to design more effective AI algorithms and interpret AI-generated insights. Understanding cybersecurity is essential for ensuring that AI systems are secure and resilient against threats, while knowledge of user experience can guide the development of AI applications that are intuitive and user-friendly.

Interdisciplinary collaboration also fosters innovation by bringing together diverse perspectives and expertise. Engineers can work with professionals from other fields to identify new opportunities for AI integration and develop solutions that address complex, real-world problems. For example, collaborating with healthcare professionals can lead to the creation of AI-driven tools that improve patient care and streamline medical processes.

To stay competitive, engineers should actively seek opportunities for interdisciplinary learning and collaboration. This can involve participating in cross-functional teams, attending industry conferences, and engaging in continuous education programs. By embracing a multidisciplinary approach, engineers can enhance their skills, stay abreast of the latest developments, and contribute to the advancement of AI technology in meaningful ways.

Chapter summary:

AI is transforming the software engineering landscape, automating routine tasks and opening up new opportunities. By focusing on creativity, problem-solving, and continuous learning, engineers can adapt to these changes and thrive in an evolving industry. Embracing AI as a tool rather than a threat will enable engineers to enhance their work, explore new career paths, and continue to drive technological innovation.

Chapter 4

Chapter 4

Navigating the Changing Landscape: Adapting to AI in Software Engineering

Introduction

As AI technology continues to advance, software engineers face a rapidly evolving landscape that demands adaptation and resilience. The integration of AI into software development brings both challenges and opportunities. This chapter explores strategies for navigating this changing environment, equipping engineers with the tools and mindset needed to thrive in an AI-enhanced world.

Embracing a Growth Mindset

To successfully adapt to AI's impact on software engineering, adopting a growth mindset is crucial. A growth mindset involves viewing challenges as opportunities for learning and development. Here's how software engineers can embrace this mindset:

- **Continuous Learning**: AI technology evolves rapidly, so staying updated with the latest trends, tools, and techniques is essential. Engineers should seek out training opportunities, online courses, and industry conferences to expand their knowledge and skills.

- **Experimentation and Innovation**: Embracing a growth mindset encourages experimentation with new technologies and methodologies. Engineers should be open to trying new AI tools, exploring innovative approaches, and pushing the boundaries of their expertise.

Developing AI Literacy

Understanding AI and its applications is vital for software engineers looking to stay relevant. Here's how to build AI literacy:

- **Learn the Basics of AI**: Start with the fundamentals of AI, including machine learning, deep learning, and natural language processing. Familiarize yourself with key concepts and technologies to better understand how they can be applied in software development.

- **Hands-On Experience**: Engage in hands-on projects involving AI to gain practical experience. Building AI models, working with AI frameworks, and integrating AI into applications will enhance your skills and confidence.

- **Collaborate with AI Experts**: Partner with colleagues or experts in the AI field to learn from their experiences and insights. Collaborative projects and discussions can provide valuable perspectives and accelerate your AI learning journey.

Leveraging AI for Efficiency

AI can significantly enhance software development processes by increasing efficiency and productivity. Here's how to leverage AI effectively:

- **Automate Routine Tasks**: Use AI tools to automate repetitive tasks such as code generation, testing, and debugging. This will free up time for engineers to focus on more complex and creative aspects of their work.

- **Optimize Development Workflows**: Implement AI-powered tools to streamline development workflows. For example, AI-driven project management software can help with task prioritization, resource allocation, and deadline management.

- **Enhance Decision-Making**: Utilize AI to analyze data and provide insights that inform decision-making. AI can help identify patterns, predict outcomes, and optimize software performance based on real-time data.

Fostering Collaboration Between Humans and AI

The successful integration of AI into software development requires effective collaboration between human engineers and AI systems. Here's how to foster this collaboration:

- **Define Clear Roles and Responsibilities**: Clearly delineate the roles and responsibilities of human engineers and AI systems. AI can handle routine tasks and data analysis, while engineers focus on creativity, problem-solving, and decision-making.

- **Integrate AI into Development Processes**: Incorporate AI tools into existing development processes to enhance efficiency and effectiveness. Ensure that AI tools complement and support the work of human engineers rather than replace them.

- **Encourage Open Communication**: Foster open communication between engineers and AI systems. Provide feedback on AI performance, share insights on system limitations, and collaborate on improving AI tools to better meet project needs.

Addressing Ethical and Social Implications

As AI becomes more integrated into software development, addressing ethical and social implications is crucial. Consider the following:

- **Privacy and Security**: Ensure that AI applications adhere to privacy and security standards. Implement measures to protect user data and prevent unauthorized access or misuse of AI technologies.

- **Bias and Fairness**: Be mindful of potential biases in AI algorithms and strive to develop fair and inclusive solutions. Regularly evaluate AI systems for fairness and take steps to mitigate any unintended biases.

- **Impact on Employment**: Consider the broader impact of AI on employment within the software engineering field. While AI may automate certain tasks, it also creates new job opportunities and areas for specialization.

Personal Stories and Case Studies

Take the story of Daniel, a software engineer who successfully adapted to AI advancements. Daniel integrated AI tools into his development process, automating routine tasks and enhancing efficiency. By learning about AI and collaborating with experts, Daniel was able to lead innovative projects and advance his career.

Quotes and References

"Adaptability is about the powerful difference between adapting to cope and adapting to win," says John C. Maxwell, a leadership expert. This quote emphasizes the importance of adapting proactively to thrive in a changing environment.

Reflection Questions

How can software engineers develop a growth mindset to adapt to the rapid advancements in AI technology?

Developing a growth mindset is essential for software engineers to adapt to the rapid advancements in AI technology. A growth mindset involves viewing challenges as opportunities for learning and development rather than as obstacles. To cultivate this mindset, engineers should start by embracing continuous learning. This means actively seeking out new knowledge and skills through various channels such as online courses, workshops, industry conferences, and professional certifications. Staying updated with the latest trends and advancements in AI technology is crucial for remaining relevant in the field.

Experimentation and innovation are also key components of a growth mindset. Engineers should be open to trying new AI tools and methodologies, even if it means stepping out of their comfort zones. By experimenting with different approaches and technologies, engineers can discover innovative solutions and improve their problem-solving abilities. Additionally, engineers should view failures and setbacks as valuable learning experiences. Instead of being discouraged by mistakes, they should analyze what went wrong, learn from it, and apply those lessons to future projects.

Networking and collaboration with peers and experts in the field can further enhance a growth mindset. Engaging in discussions, sharing knowledge, and seeking feedback from others can provide new perspectives and insights. Engineers should also set personal and professional goals that challenge them to grow and improve continuously. By maintaining a positive attitude towards learning and development, software engineers can effectively adapt to the ever-evolving landscape of AI technology.

What are some practical ways for software engineers to build AI literacy and gain hands-on experience with AI tools?

Building AI literacy and gaining hands-on experience with AI tools are crucial steps for software engineers looking to stay relevant in an AI-driven industry. One practical way to start is by learning the basics of AI, including key concepts such as machine learning, deep learning, and natural language processing. There are numerous online resources, including tutorials, courses, and textbooks, that can provide a solid foundation in these areas.

Engaging in hands-on projects is another effective way to build AI literacy. Engineers can start by working on small-scale projects that involve building and training AI models. This hands-on experience allows them to apply theoretical knowledge in practical scenarios, deepening their understanding of AI technologies. Participating in hackathons, coding competitions, and open-source projects can also provide valuable opportunities to work with AI tools and collaborate with other engineers.

Collaborating with AI experts and professionals from related fields can further enhance AI literacy. Engineers can seek mentorship, join AI-focused communities, and participate in collaborative projects to learn from the experiences and insights of others. Additionally, staying updated with the latest research papers, industry reports, and AI-related news can help engineers keep abreast of new developments and emerging trends in the field.

Finally, engineers should consider pursuing formal education in AI, such as advanced degrees or specialized certifications. These programs often provide comprehensive training and access to cutting-edge research, equipping engineers with the skills and knowledge needed to excel in AI-driven roles.

How can effective collaboration between human engineers and AI systems enhance productivity and innovation in software development?

Effective collaboration between human engineers and AI systems can significantly enhance productivity and innovation in software development. One way this collaboration can be achieved is by clearly defining the roles and responsibilities of both human engineers and AI systems. AI can handle routine and repetitive tasks, such as code generation, testing, and debugging, allowing human engineers to focus on more complex and creative aspects of their work. This division of labor ensures that each party is utilized to its strengths, maximizing overall efficiency.

Integrating AI tools into existing development processes can streamline workflows and improve productivity. For example, AI-driven project management software can help with task prioritization, resource allocation, and deadline management, enabling teams to work more effectively. AI-powered code editors can provide real-time suggestions and error detection, speeding up the coding process and reducing the likelihood of mistakes.

Collaboration between human engineers and AI systems also fosters innovation by combining the strengths of both parties. AI can analyze large datasets and identify patterns that may not be immediately apparent to humans, providing valuable insights that can inform decision-making and drive innovation. Human engineers, on the other hand, bring creativity, intuition, and contextual understanding to the table, enabling them to develop novel solutions and approaches that AI alone cannot achieve.

Open communication and feedback are essential for successful collaboration. Engineers should regularly provide feedback on AI performance, share insights on system limitations, and collaborate on improving AI tools to better meet project needs. By fostering a culture of collaboration and continuous improvement, software development teams can leverage the full potential of AI to enhance productivity and drive innovation.

Chapter Summary:

Navigating the changing landscape of software engineering in an AI-driven world requires adaptability, continuous learning, and effective collaboration. By embracing a growth mindset, developing AI literacy, leveraging AI for efficiency, and addressing ethical considerations, software engineers can thrive in this evolving environment. The future of software engineering is bright for those who are proactive, innovative, and committed to integrating AI as a powerful ally in their work.

Chapter 5

Chapter 5

Building a Collaborative Future: Humans and AI Working Together

Introduction

The future of software engineering is not about humans versus AI but about humans and AI working together to achieve greater heights. As AI continues to evolve, integrating its capabilities with human skills and creativity is essential for innovation and progress. This chapter explores how to build a collaborative future where AI and human engineers complement each other, enhance productivity, and drive technological advancements.

The Synergy of Human and AI Collaboration

Successful collaboration between humans and AI involves leveraging the strengths of both to create a more effective and innovative development process. Here's how to foster this synergy:

- **Complementary Strengths**: AI excels in tasks that involve data processing, pattern recognition, and automation. Humans bring creativity, emotional intelligence, and complex problem-solving skills. By understanding and utilizing these complementary strengths, teams can achieve more than either could alone.

- **Enhanced Problem-Solving**: Combining human intuition with AI's analytical power can lead to more effective problem-solving. AI can quickly identify patterns and provide data-driven insights, while humans can apply their creativity and judgment to interpret and act on these insights in innovative ways.

- **Augmented Decision-Making**: AI can support decision-making by providing accurate data and predictive analytics. Human engineers can then use this information to make informed decisions, considering broader contextual factors and ethical implications that AI alone cannot address.

Implementing AI-Human Collaboration Strategies

To effectively implement AI-human collaboration, consider the following strategies:

- **Integrate AI into Development Workflows**: Incorporate AI tools into existing development workflows to enhance efficiency and productivity. For example, use AI-powered code reviews to identify potential issues early in the development process, allowing engineers to focus on more complex tasks.

- **Encourage Cross-Disciplinary Teams**: Form teams that include both AI experts and software engineers. This cross-disciplinary approach fosters collaboration, enables knowledge sharing, and ensures that AI tools are effectively utilized to support development goals.

- **Provide Training and Support**: Offer training and support to help engineers understand and effectively use AI tools. This includes providing resources on AI concepts, hands-on experience with AI technologies, and ongoing support for integrating AI into their work.

Challenges and Solutions in AI-Human Collaboration

While collaboration between humans and AI offers numerous benefits, it also presents challenges that need to be addressed:

- **Communication Gaps**: Ensuring clear communication between AI systems and human engineers is crucial. Define the roles and expectations for both parties, and provide feedback mechanisms to improve AI performance and integration.

- **Trust and Reliability**: Building trust in AI systems requires demonstrating their reliability and accuracy. Implement robust testing and validation procedures to ensure that AI tools perform as expected and provide reliable results.

- **Ethical Considerations**: Address ethical considerations related to AI use, such as data privacy, bias, and fairness. Develop guidelines and best practices to ensure that AI is used responsibly and aligns with ethical standards.

Case Studies of Successful Collaboration

Consider the example of a development team at a major tech company that integrated AI into their project management process. By using AI tools to analyze project data, identify potential risks, and optimize resource allocation, the team was able to improve project outcomes and efficiency. This collaboration allowed the engineers to focus on strategic planning and innovation while AI handled routine data analysis tasks.

Quotes and References

"Technology is best when it brings people together," says Matt Mullenweg, founder of WordPress. This quote highlights the importance of technology, including AI, in enhancing human collaboration and connection.

Reflection Questions

How can software engineers integrate AI tools into their current projects to enhance collaboration and productivity?

Integrating AI tools into current projects can significantly enhance collaboration and productivity for software engineers. To begin with, engineers should identify specific areas within their projects where AI can add the most value. This might include automating repetitive tasks such as code generation, bug detection, and testing. By using AI-powered code editors and automated testing frameworks, engineers can streamline these processes, allowing them to focus on more complex and creative aspects of their work.

Next, it is essential to incorporate AI tools into the existing development workflows. This can be achieved by integrating AI-driven project management software that helps with task prioritization, resource allocation, and deadline management. Such tools can provide real-time insights and predictive analytics, enabling teams to make informed decisions and optimize their workflows. Additionally, AI-powered code reviews can identify potential issues early in the development process, ensuring higher code quality and reducing the time spent on debugging.

To foster effective collaboration, engineers should form cross-disciplinary teams that include both AI experts and software developers. This approach encourages knowledge sharing and ensures that AI tools are utilized effectively to support development goals. Providing training and support for engineers to understand and use AI tools is also crucial. This includes offering resources on AI concepts, hands-on experience with AI technologies, and ongoing support for integrating AI into their work. By equipping engineers with the necessary skills and knowledge, they can leverage AI tools to enhance their productivity and collaboration.

What strategies can software engineers implement to address challenges and build trust in AI systems?

Addressing challenges and building trust in AI systems requires a multifaceted approach. One of the primary challenges is ensuring clear communication between AI systems and human engineers. To overcome this, it is essential to define the roles and expectations for both parties clearly. Engineers should establish feedback mechanisms to continuously monitor and improve AI performance and integration. Regularly reviewing and refining these processes can help bridge communication gaps and ensure that AI tools are effectively supporting the development goals.

Building trust in AI systems also involves demonstrating their reliability and accuracy. Engineers should implement robust testing and validation procedures to ensure that AI tools perform as expected and provide reliable results. This includes conducting thorough testing under various conditions and scenarios to identify potential issues and address them proactively. Transparency is key; engineers should document their methodologies and be open about the limitations and potential biases of their AI models.

Ethical considerations are another critical aspect of building trust in AI systems. Engineers must address issues related to data privacy, bias, and fairness. Developing guidelines and best practices for responsible AI use can help ensure that AI tools align with ethical standards. This includes implementing measures to protect user data, regularly evaluating AI systems for fairness, and taking steps to mitigate any unintended biases. By prioritizing ethical considerations, engineers can build trust in AI systems and ensure their responsible use.

How can combining human intuition with AI's analytical power lead to more effective problem-solving and innovation?

Combining human intuition with AI's analytical power can lead to more effective problem-solving and innovation by leveraging the complementary strengths of both. AI excels in tasks that involve data processing, pattern recognition, and automation. It can quickly analyze large datasets, identify patterns, and provide data-driven insights that might not be immediately apparent to humans. These insights can inform decision-making and help engineers identify potential solutions to complex problems.

Human intuition, on the other hand, brings creativity, emotional intelligence, and contextual understanding to the table. Engineers can apply their creativity and judgment to interpret AI-generated insights and develop innovative solutions. For example, while AI can identify trends in user behavior, human engineers can use their understanding of user needs and preferences to design features that enhance the user experience. This combination of analytical power and human intuition can lead to more effective and user-centric solutions.

Moreover, augmented decision-making is another area where this synergy can be beneficial. AI can provide accurate data and predictive analytics, supporting engineers in making informed decisions. Human engineers can then consider broader contextual factors and ethical implications that AI alone cannot address. This holistic approach ensures that decisions are not only data-driven but also aligned with ethical standards and user needs.

In summary, by combining human intuition with AI's analytical power, software engineers can enhance their problem-solving capabilities and drive innovation. This collaborative approach leverages the strengths of both humans and AI, leading to more effective and innovative solutions in software development.

Chapter Summary:

Building a collaborative future where humans and AI work together requires a thoughtful approach to integrating AI capabilities with human skills. By understanding the complementary strengths of both, implementing effective collaboration strategies, and addressing challenges proactively, software engineers can create a more productive and innovative development environment. Embracing AI as a partner rather than a competitor will lead to exciting advancements and a brighter future for software engineering.

Chapter 6

Chapter 6

Embracing Change: How Software Engineers Can Thrive in an AI-Driven World

Introduction

As AI technology reshapes the software engineering landscape, embracing change becomes crucial for career growth and success. This chapter explores practical strategies for software engineers to not only adapt to but thrive in an AI-driven world. By focusing on continuous learning, leveraging AI effectively, and cultivating a forward-thinking mindset, engineers can position themselves for long-term success in this evolving field.

1. Cultivating a Continuous Learning Mindset

In an era of rapid technological advancement, staying updated with the latest trends and tools is essential. Here's how engineers can foster a culture of continuous learning:

- **Pursue Ongoing Education**: Enroll in online courses, attend workshops, and participate in industry conferences to stay abreast of new developments in AI and software engineering. Platforms like Coursera, Udacity, and edX offer valuable courses on AI, machine learning, and related topics.

- **Engage with Professional Communities**: Join professional organizations and online communities related to software engineering and AI. Engage in discussions, share knowledge, and learn from peers and experts in the field.

- **Seek Certifications and Specializations**: Obtain certifications in AI, machine learning, or related areas to enhance your credentials and demonstrate your expertise. Certifications from recognized institutions can validate your skills and open up new career opportunities.

2. Leveraging AI Tools to Enhance Productivity

AI tools can significantly enhance productivity and streamline workflows. Here's how to effectively leverage AI in your work:

- **Automate Repetitive Tasks**: Use AI to automate routine tasks such as code generation, bug detection, and testing. This allows you to focus on more strategic and creative aspects of software development.

- **Optimize Development Processes**: Implement AI-powered tools for project management, code review, and performance monitoring. AI can help identify inefficiencies, predict potential issues, and suggest improvements, leading to more efficient development processes.

- **Utilize AI for Personalization**: Incorporate AI into user experience design to create personalized software solutions. AI can analyze user data to tailor features, recommendations, and interactions, enhancing user satisfaction and engagement.

3. Developing Adaptability and Resilience

Adaptability and resilience are key traits for thriving in an AI-driven world. Here's how to build these qualities:

- **Embrace Change Positively**: View technological changes as opportunities rather than threats. Approach new tools and methodologies with an open mind and a willingness to learn.

- **Build Problem-Solving Skills**: Strengthen your problem-solving abilities by tackling diverse and complex challenges. Developing a strong problem-solving mindset will help you navigate the uncertainties of an evolving industry.

- **Foster a Growth-Oriented Culture**: Encourage a culture of experimentation and innovation within your team. Support colleagues in exploring new technologies and approaches, and celebrate successes and lessons learned.

4. Networking and Building Professional Relationships

Networking and building strong professional relationships can provide valuable support and open doors to new opportunities. Here's how to network effectively:

- **Attend Industry Events**: Participate in industry events, conferences, and meetups to connect with peers, industry leaders, and potential collaborators. Networking events provide opportunities to learn from others and share your own insights.

- **Engage in Online Communities**: Join online forums, discussion groups, and social media communities related to software engineering and AI. Engage in conversations, ask questions, and offer advice to build your professional network.

- **Seek Mentorship and Collaboration**: Find mentors who can provide guidance and support as you navigate your career. Collaborate with colleagues and industry experts on projects and initiatives to expand your skills and knowledge.

5. Preparing for Future Trends and Innovations

Staying ahead of future trends and innovations can give you a competitive edge. Here's how to prepare for the future of software engineering:

- **Monitor Emerging Technologies**: Keep an eye on emerging technologies and trends in AI, such as advancements in natural language processing, computer vision, and autonomous systems. Understanding these trends will help you anticipate changes and opportunities in the field.

- **Explore Interdisciplinary Applications**: Investigate how AI intersects with other fields, such as healthcare, finance, and robotics. Exploring interdisciplinary applications can uncover new areas of interest and career opportunities.

- **Plan for Long-Term Career Growth**: Set career goals and create a plan for achieving them. Consider how you can leverage AI and other technologies to advance your career and pursue new opportunities.

Case Studies and Personal Stories

Consider the example of Maria, a software engineer who embraced AI to advance her career. Maria actively pursued certifications in AI and machine learning, integrated AI tools into her development projects, and built a strong professional network. Her proactive approach allowed her to stay ahead of industry trends and take on leadership roles in innovative projects.

Quotes and References

"Change is the only constant in life," says Heraclitus, a Greek philosopher. This quote underscores the inevitability of change and the importance of adapting to thrive in an ever-evolving field.

Reflection Questions

How can software engineers incorporate continuous learning into their professional routine?

Incorporating continuous learning into a professional routine is essential for software engineers to stay updated with the latest advancements in AI and software engineering. One effective approach is to pursue ongoing education through various platforms that offer courses on AI, machine learning, and related topics. Websites like Coursera, Udacity, and edX provide a wide range of courses that can help engineers expand their knowledge and skills. Enrolling in these courses and setting aside dedicated time each week for study can ensure that learning becomes a regular part of their routine.

Engaging with professional communities is another valuable strategy. By joining organizations and online forums related to software engineering and AI, engineers can participate in discussions, share knowledge, and learn from peers and experts in the field. These communities often host webinars, workshops, and conferences that provide opportunities for continuous learning and networking. Actively participating in these events can help engineers stay informed about the latest trends and best practices.

Seeking certifications and specializations is also beneficial. Obtaining certifications in AI, machine learning, or other relevant areas can enhance an engineer's credentials and demonstrate their expertise. Certifications from recognized institutions can validate their skills and open up new career opportunities. Engineers should identify certifications that align with their career goals and invest time in preparing for and obtaining these credentials.

What steps can software engineers take to effectively leverage AI tools in their projects?

To effectively leverage AI tools in their projects, software engineers should start by identifying specific areas where AI can add the most value. This might include automating repetitive tasks such as code generation, bug detection, and testing. By using AI-powered code editors and automated testing frameworks, engineers can streamline these processes, allowing them to focus on more strategic and creative aspects of software development.

Optimizing development processes with AI-powered tools is another crucial step. Engineers can implement AI-driven project management software to help with task prioritization, resource allocation, and deadline management. These tools can provide real-time insights and predictive analytics, enabling teams to make informed decisions and optimize their workflows. Additionally, AI-powered code reviews can identify potential issues early in the development process, ensuring higher code quality and reducing the time spent on debugging.

Utilizing AI for personalization can also enhance the user experience. By incorporating AI into user experience design, engineers can create personalized software solutions that cater to individual user preferences and behaviors. AI can analyze user data to tailor features, recommendations, and interactions, enhancing user satisfaction and engagement. Engineers should explore AI tools that offer these capabilities and integrate them into their projects to deliver more customized and effective solutions.

By Mohammad Zaripour

How can software engineers develop adaptability and resilience to thrive in an AI-driven world?

Developing adaptability and resilience is crucial for software engineers to thrive in an AI-driven world. One way to build these qualities is by embracing change positively. Engineers should view technological changes as opportunities rather than threats and approach new tools and methodologies with an open mind and a willingness to learn. This positive attitude towards change can help engineers stay motivated and proactive in adapting to new developments.

Building problem-solving skills is another important aspect of developing adaptability and resilience. Engineers should strengthen their problem-solving abilities by tackling diverse and complex challenges. This can involve working on different types of projects, experimenting with new technologies, and seeking out opportunities to solve real-world problems. Developing a strong problem-solving mindset will help engineers navigate the uncertainties of an evolving industry and find innovative solutions to emerging challenges.

Fostering a growth-oriented culture within their teams can also support adaptability and resilience. Engineers should encourage a culture of experimentation and innovation, where colleagues are supported in exploring new technologies and approaches. Celebrating successes and lessons learned from failures can create an environment where continuous improvement is valued. By promoting a growth mindset and a collaborative culture, engineers can build the resilience needed to thrive in an AI-driven world.

Chapter Summary:

Thriving in an AI-driven world requires a proactive approach to continuous learning, adaptability, and effective collaboration. By leveraging AI tools, building professional relationships, and preparing for future trends, software engineers can navigate the changing landscape with confidence and success. Embracing change as an opportunity rather than a challenge will lead to a fulfilling and dynamic career in software engineering.

By Mohammad Zaripour

Chapter 7

By Mohammad Zaripour

Chapter 7

The Human Element: Why Soft Skills Are Still Crucial in an AI-Driven World

Introduction

While AI technology continues to advance, the importance of soft skills in software engineering cannot be overstated. As AI handles more technical tasks, human qualities such as communication, empathy, and teamwork become increasingly vital. This chapter explores why soft skills remain crucial in an AI-driven world and how software engineers can develop and leverage these skills to enhance their careers and work environments.

1. The Value of Communication Skills

Effective communication is essential for collaboration, project management, and stakeholder engagement. Here's why it matters:

- **Clear Articulation of Ideas**: Communicating complex technical concepts in a clear and understandable way helps bridge the gap between technical and non-technical stakeholders. This ability ensures that everyone involved in a project understands the goals, challenges, and progress.

- **Facilitation of Team Collaboration**: Strong communication skills are key to successful team dynamics. Engineers must be able to share information, provide feedback, and collaborate effectively with colleagues, clients, and other stakeholders.

- **Conflict Resolution**: Effective communication is crucial for resolving conflicts and addressing misunderstandings. Engineers with strong communication skills can navigate disagreements, negotiate solutions, and maintain positive working relationships.

2. Empathy and Emotional Intelligence

Empathy and emotional intelligence (EI) are increasingly important in an AI-enhanced work environment. Here's how these skills contribute to success:

- **Understanding User Needs**: Empathy helps engineers design software solutions that address real user needs and preferences. By understanding the user's perspective, engineers can create more intuitive and user-friendly applications.

- **Building Strong Relationships**: Emotional intelligence enables engineers to build strong relationships with colleagues and stakeholders. Understanding and responding to the emotions and needs of others fosters a positive and supportive work environment.

- **Managing Stress and Change**: Emotional intelligence helps engineers manage stress and adapt to change more effectively. By recognizing and addressing their own emotions and those of others, engineers can navigate the challenges of an evolving industry with resilience.

3. Teamwork and Collaboration

Collaboration and teamwork are essential for achieving project goals and fostering innovation. Here's why these skills matter:

- **Cross-Disciplinary Collaboration**: Software development often involves working with professionals from various disciplines, including designers, product managers, and business analysts. Effective teamwork ensures that different perspectives are integrated and that projects move forward smoothly.

- **Knowledge Sharing**: Collaborative environments encourage knowledge sharing and collective problem-solving. Engineers who excel in teamwork contribute to a culture of continuous learning and innovation.

- **Leveraging Diverse Skills**: Successful teams leverage the diverse skills and expertise of their members. Engineers who are adept at collaborating can harness the strengths of their teammates to achieve better outcomes.

4. Adaptability and Flexibility

In a rapidly changing industry, adaptability and flexibility are critical. Here's how these skills benefit engineers:

- **Embracing New Technologies**: Adaptability enables engineers to embrace and learn new technologies, including AI tools and methodologies. Being open to change helps engineers stay relevant and competitive in the evolving tech landscape.

- **Handling Unexpected Challenges**: Flexibility allows engineers to respond effectively to unexpected challenges and changes in project scope. Engineers who can adapt quickly are better equipped to handle uncertainties and maintain project momentum.

- **Continuous Improvement**: Adaptability fosters a mindset of continuous improvement. Engineers who are willing to experiment, learn from failures, and adjust their approaches contribute to ongoing personal and professional growth.

5. Leadership and Mentorship

Leadership and mentorship skills are valuable for career advancement and team development. Here's how these skills contribute to success:

- **Guiding and Inspiring Others**: Strong leadership skills help engineers guide and inspire their teams. Effective leaders set clear goals, provide support, and motivate their colleagues to achieve their best.

- **Mentoring and Developing Talent**: Mentorship allows experienced engineers to share their knowledge and support the growth of junior colleagues. By mentoring others, engineers contribute to the development of the next generation of professionals and strengthen their own leadership abilities.

- **Fostering a Positive Work Culture**: Leadership and mentorship contribute to a positive and productive work culture. Engineers who lead by example and support their colleagues create a collaborative and inclusive environment.

6. Building and Maintaining Professional Relationships

Strong professional relationships are crucial for career growth and success. Here's how to build and maintain these relationships:

- **Networking**: Engage with industry peers, attend events, and participate in professional communities to build a strong network. Networking opens up opportunities for collaboration, career advancement, and knowledge sharing.

- **Maintaining Connections**: Stay in touch with former colleagues, mentors, and industry contacts. Regularly check in and offer support to maintain and strengthen professional relationships.

- **Professionalism and Respect**: Demonstrate professionalism and respect in all interactions. Building a reputation for reliability, integrity, and respect enhances your professional relationships and career prospects.

Case Studies and Personal Stories

Consider the story of Alex, a software engineer who excelled in both technical and soft skills. Alex's strong communication, empathy, and teamwork abilities helped him lead successful projects and build lasting professional relationships. His ability to adapt to new technologies and mentor junior engineers contributed to his career growth and the success of his team.

Quotes and References

"Soft skills are the new hard skills," says Daniel Goleman, author of *Emotional Intelligence*. This quote highlights the increasing importance of soft skills in a technology-driven world and their role in achieving professional success.

Reflection Questions

How can software engineers improve their communication skills to enhance collaboration and project success?

Improving communication skills is essential for software engineers to enhance collaboration and project success. One effective way to start is by practicing clear and concise articulation of ideas. Engineers should focus on explaining complex technical concepts in a way that is understandable to non-technical stakeholders. This involves breaking down technical jargon into simpler terms and using analogies or visual aids to illustrate key points. Regularly presenting ideas to diverse audiences, such as team meetings or client presentations, can help engineers refine their communication skills and build confidence.

Active listening is another crucial aspect of effective communication. Engineers should practice listening attentively to their colleagues, clients, and stakeholders, ensuring they fully understand their perspectives and concerns. This involves asking clarifying questions, summarizing key points, and providing thoughtful responses. By actively listening, engineers can foster better collaboration, address misunderstandings, and build stronger relationships.

Written communication is equally important. Engineers should work on improving their writing skills by crafting clear and well-structured emails, reports, and documentation. This includes paying attention to grammar, punctuation, and formatting to ensure that written communication is professional and easy to understand. Seeking feedback from peers and mentors on written communication can provide valuable insights and help engineers improve their writing style.

What steps can software engineers take to develop and apply emotional intelligence in their work environment?

Developing and applying emotional intelligence (EI) in the work environment involves several key steps. First, engineers should focus on self-awareness, which is the ability to recognize and understand their own emotions. This can be achieved through regular self-reflection, mindfulness practices, and seeking feedback from others. By becoming more aware of their emotional responses, engineers can better manage their emotions and respond more effectively to challenging situations.

Empathy is another critical component of EI. Engineers can develop empathy by actively seeking to understand the emotions and perspectives of their colleagues, clients, and users. This involves listening with an open mind, asking questions to gain deeper insights, and showing genuine concern for others' well-being. Practicing empathy helps engineers build stronger relationships, foster a supportive work environment, and design user-centric solutions.

Effective emotion regulation is also essential. Engineers should learn techniques for managing stress and maintaining emotional balance, such as deep breathing exercises, taking breaks, and engaging in physical activities. By managing their emotions effectively, engineers can remain calm and composed under pressure, make better decisions, and maintain positive interactions with others.

How can software engineers leverage teamwork and collaboration to achieve project goals and foster innovation?

Leveraging teamwork and collaboration is crucial for software engineers to achieve project goals and foster innovation. One way to enhance teamwork is by promoting a culture of open communication and knowledge sharing. Engineers should encourage team members to share their ideas, insights, and feedback openly. This can be facilitated through regular team meetings, brainstorming sessions, and collaborative tools such as project management software and communication platforms.

Cross-disciplinary collaboration is also vital. Software development often involves working with professionals from various disciplines, including designers, product managers, and business analysts. Engineers should actively seek to understand the perspectives and expertise of their colleagues from different fields. By integrating diverse viewpoints, teams can develop more comprehensive and innovative solutions.

Building trust and mutual respect within the team is essential for effective collaboration. Engineers should demonstrate reliability, integrity, and respect in their interactions with colleagues. This involves meeting deadlines, delivering high-quality work, and acknowledging the contributions of others. By fostering a positive and inclusive team environment, engineers can enhance collaboration and drive collective success.

Encouraging a growth mindset within the team can further promote innovation. Engineers should support their colleagues in exploring new technologies, experimenting with different approaches, and learning from failures. Celebrating successes and lessons learned from challenges can create a culture of continuous improvement and innovation. By leveraging the strengths and expertise of their team members, engineers can achieve project goals more effectively and drive technological advancements.

Chapter Summary:

In an AI-driven world, soft skills such as communication, empathy, teamwork, and adaptability remain crucial for success in software engineering. By developing and leveraging these skills, engineers can enhance their careers, build strong professional relationships, and contribute to a positive and innovative work environment. Embracing the human element alongside technological advancements will lead to a more balanced and fulfilling career in software engineering.

By Mohammad Zaripour

Conclusion

Conclusion:

As we conclude our exploration of how AI impacts the world of software engineering, it's clear that while the landscape is evolving, the core principles of successful engineering remain steadfast. The integration of AI into software development presents both opportunities and challenges, and navigating this new terrain requires a blend of technical expertise and essential soft skills.

Embracing Change

The rise of AI brings profound changes to the software engineering field, but it also opens up new avenues for innovation and growth.

Embracing these changes with a proactive mindset is key to thriving in an AI-driven world. By viewing AI as a tool that complements rather than replaces human skills, engineers can harness its capabilities to enhance their work, drive efficiency, and unlock new possibilities.

Continuous Learning and Adaptability

Continuous learning is no longer optional; it's a necessity. The rapid pace of technological advancement means that staying updated with the latest developments in AI and software engineering is crucial. Engineers who commit to ongoing education, seek out new challenges, and adapt to evolving tools and methodologies will remain at the forefront of the industry.

The Power of Collaboration

Effective collaboration between humans and AI is essential for achieving the best outcomes. By understanding the complementary strengths of both, engineers can leverage AI to handle routine tasks and data analysis while applying their creativity, problem-solving skills, and emotional intelligence to drive innovation and maintain strong team dynamics.

Soft Skills in an AI-Driven World

Despite the rise of AI, soft skills such as communication, empathy, and teamwork are more important than ever. These human qualities enhance collaboration, build strong relationships, and contribute to a positive work environment. Engineers who develop and apply these skills alongside their technical expertise will find themselves well-positioned for success.

Preparing for the Future

Looking ahead, the ability to anticipate future trends and prepare for new developments will set successful engineers apart. By staying informed about emerging technologies, exploring interdisciplinary applications, and setting long-term career goals, engineers can navigate the future with confidence and continue to make meaningful contributions to the field.

Final Thoughts

The journey through this book has highlighted the ways in which AI is transforming software engineering and the strategies for adapting to this change. While AI will undoubtedly continue to shape the industry, it is the combination of technical prowess and human skills that will define success. Embrace the opportunities that AI presents, invest in continuous learning, foster effective collaboration, and cultivate the soft skills that will drive your career forward.

In conclusion, the future of software engineering is bright and full of potential. By approaching AI with curiosity and resilience, and by valuing both technological and human contributions, you will be well-equipped to thrive in an ever-evolving industry. The path ahead is not just about adapting to change but also about leading the way in shaping the future of technology.

By Mohammad Zaripour

Appendix

Appendix

Resources, Tools, and Further Reading

This appendix provides a comprehensive collection of resources, tools, and further reading to support and expand upon the topics covered in the book. It includes recommended books, online courses, professional organizations, and tools for both software engineering and AI, offering valuable references for continued learning and professional development.

A. Recommended Books

1. **On AI and Technology**

- *Artificial Intelligence: A Guide for Thinking Humans* by Melanie Mitchell
  This book offers a comprehensive overview of AI, its capabilities, and its limitations, providing insights into the future of artificial intelligence.

- *The Fourth Industrial Revolution* by Klaus Schwab
  Schwab explores the transformative impact of the Fourth Industrial Revolution, including the role of AI and other emerging technologies in shaping the future of work.

- *AI Superpowers: China, Silicon Valley, and the New World Order* by Kai-Fu Lee
  This book provides a comparative analysis of AI development in China and the U.S., offering valuable insights into the global landscape of artificial intelligence.

2. **On Software Engineering**

    - *Clean Code: A Handbook of Agile Software Craftsmanship* by Robert C.

Martin
Martin's classic work on software development emphasizes best practices for writing clean, maintainable code.

- *The Pragmatic Programmer: Your Journey To Mastery* by Andrew Hunt and David Thomas
  This book provides practical advice and strategies for software development, focusing on practical techniques for becoming a better programmer.

- *Design Patterns: Elements of Reusable Object-Oriented Software* by Erich Gamma, Richard Helm, Ralph Johnson, and John Vlissides
  A foundational text on design patterns, this book is essential for understanding reusable solutions to common software design problems.

3. **On Soft Skills and Professional Development**

    - *Emotional Intelligence 2.0* by Travis Bradberry and Jean Greaves
      This book offers insights into

developing emotional intelligence and its impact on personal and professional success.

- *How to Win Friends and Influence People* by Dale Carnegie
Carnegie's classic work on interpersonal skills and communication provides timeless strategies for building relationships and influencing others.

- *The 7 Habits of Highly Effective People* by Stephen R. Covey
Covey's principles for personal and professional effectiveness remain relevant for achieving success in a technology-driven world.

B. Online Courses and Certifications

1. AI and Machine Learning

- **Coursera**
  - *Machine Learning* by Andrew Ng
  A foundational course in machine learning, providing practical

experience with algorithms and techniques.

- *Deep Learning Specialization* by Andrew Ng
  A series of courses covering various aspects of deep learning, including neural networks, convolutional networks, and sequence models.

- **edX**

  - *AI for Everyone* by Andrew Ng
    An introductory course designed for non-technical professionals to understand the impact of AI on business and society.

  - *Artificial Intelligence MicroMasters* by Columbia University
    A comprehensive program covering AI fundamentals, machine learning, and natural language processing.

- **Udacity**
  - *AI Programming with Python Nanodegree*
    A hands-on program focusing on programming with Python and building AI applications.

  - *Deep Reinforcement Learning Nanodegree*
    An advanced program exploring reinforcement learning and its applications.

2. **Software Engineering**

- **Pluralsight**
  - *Software Architecture*
    A series of courses on software architecture principles, design patterns, and best practices.

  - *Agile Software Development*
    Courses on Agile methodologies, including Scrum and Kanban, for effective project management.

- **LinkedIn Learning**
  - *Programming Foundations*
    Courses on fundamental programming concepts and techniques.
  - *Advanced JavaScript*
    An in-depth course on advanced JavaScript concepts and practices.

3. **Soft Skills and Professional Development**

   - **Skillshare**
     - *Communication Skills for Engineers*
       Courses focused on improving communication skills tailored to technical professionals.
     - *Leadership and Management*
       Courses on developing leadership and management skills in a technology-driven environment.
   - **Coursera**

- *The Science of Well-Being* by Yale University
  A course on improving personal well-being and productivity, applicable to both professional and appendixx
- *Successful Negotiation: Essential Strategies and Skills* by University of Michigan
  A course on negotiation skills, useful for managing client relationships and team dynamics.

C. Professional Organizations and Communities

1. **Software Engineering and AI**

    - **IEEE Computer Society**
      Offers resources, conferences, and publications related to software engineering and computer science.

    - **Association for Computing Machinery (ACM)**
      Provides access to journals, conferences, and professional

development opportunities in computing and AI.

- **Artificial Intelligence (AI) Research Organizations**
  - *OpenAI*
    A research organization focused on developing and promoting friendly AI for the benefit of humanity.
  - *DeepMind*
    A leading AI research lab known for its work in reinforcement learning and artificial general intelligence.

2. **Networking and Career Development**

  - **LinkedIn Groups**
    - *Software Engineering Community*
      A professional group for software engineers to share knowledge and network.
    - *AI and Machine Learning Professionals*
      A group for discussions on

AI trends, job opportunities, and research.

- **Meetup**
  - *Tech Meetups*
    Local tech meetups provide opportunities for networking, learning, and collaboration in various tech fields.
  - *AI and Data Science Meetups*
    Connect with professionals and enthusiasts interested in AI and data science.

D. Tools and Resources

1. **AI Tools**

   - **TensorFlow**
     An open-source library for machine learning and deep learning applications.

   - **PyTorch**
     A deep learning framework known for its flexibility and ease of use.

   - **Keras**
     A high-level neural networks API,

written in Python and capable of running on top of TensorFlow.

2. **Software Engineering Tools**

    o **Git**
    A version control system essential for managing code changes and collaboration.

    o **JIRA**
    A popular project management tool for tracking and managing software development tasks.

    o **Docker**
    A platform for developing, shipping, and running applications in containers.

3. **Collaboration and Communication Tools**

    o **Slack**
    A messaging platform for team communication and collaboration.

    o **Microsoft Teams**
    A collaboration tool that integrates with Office 365 and provides chat, video meetings, and file sharing.

- **Zoom**
  A video conferencing tool for virtual meetings and webinars.

E. Glossary of Terms

- **AI (Artificial Intelligence)**: The simulation of human intelligence processes by machines, especially computer systems.

- **Machine Learning**: A subset of AI that involves training algorithms to learn from and make predictions based on data.

- **Deep Learning**: A branch of machine learning involving neural networks with many layers, used for complex tasks such as image and speech recognition.

- **Emotional Intelligence (EI)**: The ability to recognize, understand, and manage one's own emotions and the emotions of others.

- **Version Control**: A system for managing changes to source code over time, allowing multiple contributors to collaborate on projects.

www.ingramcontent.com/pod-product-compliance
Lightning Source LLC
Chambersburg PA
CBHW050258230526
45471CB00005B/1934